BUILDING A BUSINESS BY BUILDING
RELATIONSHIPS

BUILDING A BUSINESS BY BUILDING RELATIONSHIPS

HOW A HEART FOR THE
MARKETPLACE CAN HELP
YOU GROW PROFITS

JIM & PAULA NEWMAN

Copyright @ 2021 Paula Newman

ISBN: 9798545274192

Cover Design by Tehsin Gull

Interior by HMD Publishing

All rights reserved

All quoted Scripture is from THE HOLY BIBLE, NEW INTERNATIONAL VERSION, NIV. Copyright 1973, 1978, 1984, 2011 by Biblica, Inc. Used by permission.

The information provided in this book is for informational purposes only and is not intended to be a source of advice with respect to the material presented. The information and/or documents contained in this book do not constitute legal or financial advice and should never be used without first consulting with a financial professional to determine what may be best for your individual needs.

The author does not make any guarantee or other promise as to any results that may be obtained from using the content of this book. You should never make any investment decision without first consulting with your own financial advisor and conducting your own research and due diligence. To the maximum extent permitted by law, the author disclaims any and all liability in the event any information, commentary, analysis, opinions, advice and/or recommendations contained in this book prove to be inaccurate, incomplete or unreliable, or result in any investment or other losses.

Content contained or made available through this book is not intended to and does not constitute legal advice or investment advice, and no attorney-client relationship is formed. The author is providing this book and its contents on an "as is" basis. Your use of the information in this book is at your own risk.

Although the author has made every effort to ensure that the information in this book was correct at press time and while this publication is designed to provide accurate information in regard to the subject matter covered, the author assumes no responsibility for errors, inaccuracies, omissions, or any other inconsistencies herein and hereby disclaims any liability to any party for any loss, damage, or disruption caused by errors or omissions, whether such errors or omissions result from negligence, accident, or any other cause.

This publication is meant as a source of valuable information for the reader, however it is not meant as a substitute for direct expert assistance. If such level of assistance is required, the services of a competent professional should be sought.

Dedication

To business owners who choose their life calling to make a lasting impact for God in the lives of those they lead.

Foreword

Who says nice guys finish last?

Jim and Paula are two of the nicest people I know. Their warmth and genuine love for people positively radiate from them. Yet, they have won numerous awards for being the first and best at what they do: running successful businesses.

For nearly 40 years, their strategy of putting people ahead of profits has consistently yielded...*more profits*. By all accounts, it has also created a more enjoyable working environment for everyone and has resulted in increased influence in every community where their doors are open for business.

In recent years, Christian business owners have finally been encouraged to believe that their role in the marketplace is a vital ministry. Let's be honest here. Most people spend far more time with co-workers or sitting in restaurants than they'll ever spend sitting in a pew.

The opportunities to be a light are endless. The question is: do we have to sacrifice profits to share the love of God? Is this an either/or proposition? Either we love God, or we grow successful businesses?

The Newmans' answer is emphatic: we can and must do both.

In ***Building a Business by Building Relationships***, the Newmans share practical strategies to help you honor God by treating people right. *(Hint: it has nothing to do with being preachy or handing out tracts.)* Here you'll find hard-fought wisdom for improving your people skills, from hiring and training employees to wise counsel about working with vendors and professionals. Plus insights on achieving work-life balance, especially if your family members work together.

It's my honor to commend to you both the authors and their message about how a heart for the marketplace can help you grow profits.

Donna Partow,
Bestselling Author, *Becoming the Woman God Wants Me To Be*

Contents

Dedication 5

Foreword 7

A Word from Jim 11

Introduction 13

Chapter 1. Relationships with People 17

Chapter 2. Relationship Health 27

Chapter 3. Relationship with Your
First Customer 35

Chapter 4. Relationship Culture of Safe Space
Communication 49

Chapter 5. Relationship Culture of
Learning Names 55

Chapter 6. Relationship with Community 65

Chapter 7. Relationship with Professionals
& Purveyors 73

Chapter 8. Relationship with God 83

Chapter 9. Relationship with Self 93

Chapter 10. Relationship with Spouse
and Family 105

Conclusion	123
Pay It Forward	125
Special Thanks from Paula	127
About Jim & Paula Newman	129

A Word from Jim

I was 19 when I first met Paula. We were in a group of eight people. It seemed to be her mission to get "quiet" Jim to talk about himself. She had friendly eyes that seemed to smile and set me at ease to talk. We all felt her genuine connection and interest in us. I was the lucky one whose connection has grown into a 45-year marriage.

What I have learned from Paula is all people are self-conscious, and all people matter. If I think about others and ask them questions, it takes the pressure off me coming up with something to say. People are more interested in talking about themselves than hearing about me anyway.

She also has shown that if you want a friend, you need to be a friend. So for business to be satisfying, it must be about relationship building. Without relationships, business is sterile.

Paula started off as a Domestic Engineer who encouraged me from the sidelines but became an integral part of our business, growing our loyal customer base. She has joined many community groups looking for what we can add while promoting our business. She is the face of our business. I smile as sometimes people ask me, "What do you do in Paula's business?" She has developed our mission statement and guiding principles. She interviews and orientates most of our employees, to begin with an empowering start. She is quick to introduce employees to customers she knows. She has increased our sales significantly. I have seen her carry her relationship messages at home and internationally.

Paula and I have been successful as a team. Do we always agree? No! But I have learned to listen to my wife. She gets it right more often than I. Especially when it comes to how people are doing or who need encouragement.

Even without knowing the ins and outs of your business, Paula can improve your customer base, employee retention, and standing in your community...simply by teaching you how to build win-win relationships.

Introduction

"God took the man and put him in the Garden of Eden to work it and take care of it."
- Genesis 2:15 NIV

"Ocean in view! O! The joy!"
- William Clark of the Lewis and Clark expedition

We all have an assignment! As an entrepreneur, the trail you've chosen to blaze is full of adventure, treacherous surprises, and a winding river through stretches of canyons leading to the mountain range you had set on climbing. It is not for the faint of heart. The risk factor is imminent. No one trailblazer makes it on their own. They need others wanting to experience the journey with them. Through those relationships built along the way, you make it to the land to claim as your own called entrepreneurship.

Welcome, fellow entrepreneur!

Are you looking to grow your business to become more influential and prosperous? If so, you've come to the right book.

You may have already invested several years and sacrificed your resources to get where you are today. It has undoubtedly taken your time, sleep, and headspace to deliver on the vision you initially saw. Your vision was filled with hope, dreams, and a little bit of naivety.

But if you're anything like me and most business owners I know, the reality may have fallen short of the dream. Does any of the following sound vaguely familiar:

- You may be stuck or unsatisfied with where the sales have been.

- You are struggling with employees who lack enthusiasm.

- The dream you shared with your spouse is lost or buried under the stress of challenges.

- You feel like you're neglecting those who are the most important to you – creating guilt, shame, and even remorse. Wondering, is it worth it?

- You are frustrated and mystified when you hear people in your community say, "I didn't even know your business was here!" Your community around you knows little about the story of how and why your business began.

- You don't feel like you have the resources to sow into the community of your business. Yet you know it's important.

Every one of these scenarios has been part of my journey in business. I know the pain, turmoil, frustrating nagging feeling of "there's got to be an answer" and "there's got to be more."

The dreams that got Jim and me into business excited us. We could make a good income providing something people needed and wanted. That is a win for them and us.

It is called the free enterprise system and has benefited our customers and allowed my family to live a life of fulfilled dreams. I have found my calling to be a Christian business owner sharing the wisdom and love of God in all I do and in every relationship.

Jim and I have owned multiple businesses simultaneously, almost from the start of our marriage. One was a newly-formed franchise. At the beginning of the franchise formation, Jim helped create products, procedures, and leadership. The ability to hire and train good managers made owning multiple stores a reality. Many of the stores grew to be in the top 10 highest volume sales of the franchise for most of the 38 years of business.

In this franchise, we have started new businesses. But we also purchased struggling stores and turned them profitable. We have occasionally partnered with others. We have held honors such as *Franchisee of the Year*, *Sales Increase of the Year,* and *Highest Sales Volume*.

It has been an honor to be named *Small Business of the Year* in two different communities. I was named *Business Leader of the Year* in another town. Jim and I have served on multiple boards in our franchise and organizations such as the Chamber of Commerce.

Now I want to help YOU achieve the same success with your business because I care! Our national economy needs every small business possible to thrive. According to the Small Business Administration, 48% of all US employees work for small businesses.   JPMorgan Chase says, *"Small businesses are an anchor of the US economy."*

Even though I don't know your name or the name of your business, I do know:

- what keeps you up at night
- what 80% of your conversations are about
- what concerns you about your employees.

Marcus Lemonis, featured on the popular TV show *The Profit*, specializes in rescuing failing businesses. He says, *"Transformation of people is usually what makes a business grow."*

Here's the entire secret: the way to build your business is by building relationships!

Are you ready to transform the people in your business – *starting with the person in the mirror* – to see your business grow? If so, you're reading the right book.

In this book, you're about to discover how to make your business dreams a reality with one simple strategy: **Building Your Business by Building Relationships**.

CHAPTER 1:
Relationships with People

"If people like you they'll listen to you, but if they trust you they'll do business with you."
- Zig Ziglar

The very nature of business is to provide a product or service to people.

People are your customers, your employees, and the service providers who keep your businesses running. People help advertise your business. Sometimes they are good advertisements (when you've done well). Sometimes the advertisements are not so good (when you miss the mark). Professional people advise you, help you with your taxes and protect your investment in the business. The people in the community either support you and become powerful business allies. Or they ignore you or even actively oppose you, which becomes a liability.

Lewis and Clark could not have made their expedition without the people skills and language expertise of Sacagawea. Packed in their gear were 50 peace pipes to clarify their intentions with people they met.

Being in business is being in the business of working with people. And that requires relationship skills. So let's start with how you think of people.

Each one of us has a different level of comfort in the process of getting to know a person. Past experiences with people, whether positive or negative, certainly are a factor. But how you think of people determines how you respond to them. I get energized around people, especially if we make a connection through something we have in common. I see almost everyone as a potential new friend I just haven't met yet.

On the other hand, my husband and business partner, Jim, is usually exhausted when he is in a group of people he doesn't know. He enjoys people when he knows them, but getting to know them can be challenging. Although we have different comfort levels in interacting with people, we've both found a way to build our business by building relationships. It's just that I go wide...and Jim goes deep.

Which one of us can you relate to? Does it excite you to meet new people or does it drain you? The good news is, whether you tend to be energized – *or drained* – there is a way forward for you.

If you don't already know your personality type, taking a personality test can be one of the first steps to helping you on this journey. Taking a personality test enabled us to identify our differences and brought our individual strengths into focus. Jim and I became an even better team, and the appreciation for our differences connected us on a deeper level.

All personalities can connect with people. The ways to connect will vary, which is wonderful because all personalities NEED different ways to connect. An introvert will tend to go deeper in the relationship and have fewer relationships than an extrovert. There's a way to win for every personality. There's a way for me, there's a way for Jim, and there's a way for YOU.

Taking a personality test will help you understand yourself and everyone around you better. As a result, your business will inevitably be strengthened.

Personality Test

The personality test I recommend for all management positions in your business is *Now Discover Your Strengths* from Gallup. It provides much insight into a person and how to relate to them in building a relationship. Gallup found 34 basic personality types and believes that your strengths are hard-wired in your brain and reveal the top 5 strengths of your personality. The tendency is to assume that everyone can do what you do because it is easy for you; however, that is not the case. If something is easy for you, then that is a strength that you should utilize and improve.

Having my employees take this test has helped me to develop people and hire for specific needs. Any business that offers a service to people needs to understand personalities and relationships. Healthy relationships, especially in the workplace environment, can provide an atmosphere for:

- Personal growth
- Long-term employment
- Loyalty to your brand
- People wanting employment in your company
- Growth of your customer base
- Community influence

The opposite is also true. Unhealthy relationship practices as employers/managers make for a miserable place to work. But it's even worse than it sounds. If they deal with the public in any capacity, unhappy employees create a place where people no longer want to give money for a service rendered. In other words, a lost customer.

People Quit Bosses

According to DDI Research, a global leadership consulting firm, 57% of employees quit because of their boss. That means frustrations with the boss drive more than half of employees out the door. An additional third stick around but dream of opportunities to get away from their manager. The article continues to say that it is the relationships and emotions of managers that are the issue. Yes, I know it's easier to blame the employees, but that's not what the research shows. #ouch

But it's not just employees quitting bosses that's the problem. The bosses are having a tough time, too. In fact, *"managers rate difficult conversations, coaching, and engaging their teams as their top challenges."*

One definition of the word relationship is *"the way in which two or more concepts, objects or people are connected, or the state of being connected."* The word connected means *"brought together or into contact so that a real or notional link is established."*

An established link! Think of being linked to someone to provide a win for them and a win for you!

Once established, the link will take regular communication to keep the link strong and vital.

Here is my personal story of a relationship with another business owner. Through building the relationship, both of us found healing *and* grew our respective businesses.

It started when my son, who is also a partner in our business, expressed concern for one of his employees. She couldn't come in for a scheduled shift because her violent boyfriend was intimidating her. She was afraid to leave the situation. He informed me that she was one of several on his staff in domestic violence relationships.

Feeling uncertain about how to help them, I called a crisis hotline. They offered shelter if she would come in. They suggested that we place stickers in the bathrooms of our restaurant with the crisis hotline number for domestic violence. But I realized that more needed to be done.

I prayed and educated myself on the subject for three days, and then I met my friend. She had a t-shirt business. Some of the shirts said, *"Sticks and stones may break my bones but sometimes words are worse."* When I asked her about the quotes, she told me her story of surviving domestic abuse. Instantly I knew we could help each other.

For 12 years, our relationship, *that established link*, has thrived. We carry each other's business cards. We often brainstorm about new products. Or discuss how to better relate to our business associates. We have joined forces many times for joint marketing events. Relationships that become authentic are life-changing for both people

The Power of Asking

How do you draw near to someone to begin building a relationship? The simplest way is just by asking a question, a question about *them*.

Asking questions builds relationships. It is how we discover commonalities. And commonalities are what begin an acquaintance. The more exposure you have to each other, the more the relationship grows. For instance, if you have a working relationship with someone and invite them to a concert together, you have expanded the relationship to include a social setting.

It is human nature to talk about ourselves. Resist that ever-present temptation and instead follow Dale Carnegie's classic advice on **How to Win Friends & Influence People**: focus on the other person. Asking questions is an easy way to get the other person to do more of the talking. Even introverts can ask questions to begin a conversation. Extroverts, in general, need to talk less and listen more. In both cases, the answer is asking more questions.

It's sad to think that people can work together without knowing much about each other, even though they spend hours together week after week. Respecting another person's privacy is essential, of course. But being a safe person *(someone who does not gossip)* is the surest way to become someone who even a private person can have a relationship with. The point is to be sensitive, *not prying*, when asking questions.

Caring about the welfare of your employees can give great meaning to work as a business owner or manager. Could that be part of the greater purpose in your work as a business owner? Could there be more to it than just making a living?

Most people who work outside their homes spend more hours in a week with the people at work than family members. So the work environment needs to be intentionally positive. A place where people can do their best at their job.

For a business to run efficiently and effectively, there need to be guidelines to accomplish that. When you create a relationship-building culture for both staff and customers, the business naturally grows. (Chapter Four goes into much greater depth about how to do just that.)

As a business owner, I know how limited your time is. I pray this book will begin a search for your surrender to God's kingdom-way of business as a God-given calling. Building relationships with your staff and business associates is a perfect place to make a difference for good.

Now Grow It

Now, Discover Your Strengths by Don Clifton

StrengthFinders Test online:

https://www.gallup.com/cliftonstrengths/en/253868/popular-cliftonstrengthsassessment-products.aspx

CHAPTER 2:
Relationship Health

"A man reaps what he sows... Let us not become weary in doing good, for at the proper time we will reap a harvest if we do not give up."
- Galatians 6:7-10

There are many relationships in the workplace. Any relationship that goes on for an extended time will be tried and tested. Relationships that are tried and tested are also satisfying. Knowing ahead of time that there will be both trials and satisfaction enables you to respond in a way that can lead to growth and stability.

Healthy things grow when they have an adequate environment. Jim and I recently put in a backyard, unlike anything we have had before. Our goal, instead of grass, was to have lots of bushes, flowers, vegetable-raised beds, and fruit trees with stone walkways for accessibility and enjoyment. We have both full sun and shade areas on our pie-shaped lot on the river. When purchasing the plants, we constantly had to identify where the plant would thrive – either in the sun or shade. The same is true with relationships in determining what will grow health in relationships.

Begin by developing an awareness of healthy and unhealthy characteristics regarding relationships. Unhealthy relationships create drama, waste time, reduce efficiency and diminish morale.

Healthy relationships create an atmosphere where employees grow as individuals and, as a result, customers want to be around them. Healthy relationships create an atmosphere of trust, cooperation, teamwork, and joy on the job.

Warning Signs of Unhealthy Relationships

Here are some key warning signs that your business might be adversely affected by unhealthy relationships:

- Continual disagreements
- Felt tension
- Little conversation about expectations
- Constant criticism
- Vague compliments such as, "Good work!" without specifics
- Using words such as, always or never *(which is shaming)*
- Blame shifting, rather than taking personal responsibility
- Lack of enthusiastic energy
- Conversations where one person does most of the talking
- Lack of eye contact
- Hostile or defensive body language

These certainly aren't all of the warning signs. But they should get the wheels turning as some issues come to light. The most important point to get is this:

STOP ALLOWING UNHEALTHY BEHAVIOR IN YOUR BUSINESS!

- It holds your business back from growing.
- People do not like coming to work in that kind of environment.
- It causes constant employee turnover.
- Customers sense the dysfunction and will choose to go elsewhere.
- The destructive behaviors continue and may even become worse

Changing from unhealthy behaviors to respectful behaviors is your new goal. This will bring about a safe environment where people are honored and respected.

You Can Shift the Atmosphere

Our bodies give off energy. It is easily understood when we talk about "the elephant in the room." Everyone feels the tension. The good news is, the same can be true of a heart filled with love. That's why I check myself before I enter the workplace to acknowledge what is top-of-mind, in my heart, or what Holy Spirit wants me to see.

Some situations can put pressure on our ability to respond peaceably. Here's how I face potentially challenging situations:

Plan → Pause → Proceed

Plan: Follow the core values and mission statement of your business.

Pause: Examine my heart to see if whether or not I am experiencing God's peace.

Proceed: Only after I have asked for wisdom and received it.

You may have to sit in your car, hide in a bathroom stall or lock the door of your office for a while. But whatever you do, make sure YOU can always be relied upon to shift the atmosphere in an uplifting, God-honoring direction. You carry the presence of God with you, and everyone around you should sense – *and benefit from* – the peace He brings.

Healthy Relationship Characteristics

Here are some healthy relationship characteristics. Pray over this list and honestly ask God if this is what people think of when they think of the work environment you have created:

- Mutual respect
- Vulnerability
- Total trust in each other
- Unwavering honesty
- Mutual empathy
- Kindness

- Healthy boundaries
- Total commitment
- Thoughtfulness
- Forgiveness
- Gentleness
- Lots of affection
- Consistent appreciation
- Every person feels validated

No business is perfect. But this is the type of atmosphere that's created when the Prince of Peace is allowed to take His rightful place. These are great checkpoints to consider when evaluating the people side of running your business.

You can choose to run a relationship-driven business. We've found that genuinely helping people, starting with the people who work for us, transformed our lives as business owners. It is also the road to making money as an entrepreneur. Building relationships *is* building a business.

"Everybody can be great...because anybody can serve. You don't have to have a college degree to serve. You don't have to make your subject and verb agree to serve. You only need a heart full of grace. A soul generated by love."
- Martin Luther King Jr.

Now Grow It:

Create a reminder to keep a loving attitude top of mind. Suggestions to choose from:

- Put a verse or quote on your phone cover.

- Write on a 3x5 card the verse or quote to carry it on you.

- Find someone to hold you accountable.

CHAPTER 3:
Relationship with Your First Customer

> *"For by the grace given me I say to every one of you: Do not think of yourself more highly than you ought, but rather think of yourself with sober judgment, in accordance with the faith God has distributed to each of you."*
> *- Romans 12:3*

Do you remember your first job?

Did you like your boss?

Were you afraid of doing something wrong and getting in trouble?

Did you feel your boss liked you?

Jim and I had bosses who liked us. We worked hard for them. Because we felt liked and appreciated, we wanted to perform to their expectations and to live up to the potential they saw in us.

Employees are essential to a business. They can be the face that the customer interacts with on a continuing basis. So to have an excellent customer service experience, the employee needs to experience great service from us, their employer. That is why we call employees "First Customers."

Seeing your employees as the First Customer means you treat them as well as *or better than* your most valued customer. When employees are greeted with a warm welcome every day, they want to come to work. Everyone wants to be seen, known, and appreciated. When everything they need to do their job well is provided – and they are appreciated and appropriately rewarded — they want to continue their employment with you.

Using the term, First Customer sets a needed mindset toward the value of an employee in your business. Building a strong, healthy relationship with your First Customer(s) will bring the second customers in regularly.

How can you build this strong, healthy relationship? Here are three keys:

1. Take notice of what your employee is doing correctly. It is far easier to look at what needs correcting. But necessary corrections will be heard if the culture is heavier on gratitude and affirmation first.

2. Be quick to affirm and appreciate what you saw that was done correctly. Be specific! Appreciating and affirming may need some practice with intentionality. I had to train myself to look for things to thank and affirm. I also had to hold the things that needed correcting until a better time. It's worth the effort because appreciation arouses enthusiasm!

3. Ask them if there is anything you can provide to make their job more efficient. An employee is often more aware of what equipment can help improve the customer's experience. Sometimes a policy is needed to get the team better synchronized.

Rewards, Celebrations & Awards

Rewards are huge! Don't underestimate how powerful they can be. The #1 management principle in the world is: What gets rewarded gets repeated!

What are you rewarding in your business?

A reward is something given when what was desired has been achieved.

A celebration is an impromptu acknowledgment of something that has been accomplished.

The difference between a reward and a celebration is how you use it, not what it is.

Here are some things to reward:

- Work effort that is above and beyond regular duties
- Outstanding performance
- Recruiting needed employees
- Bringing in new customers
- Satisfying a disgruntled customer
- Coming up with a solution to a problem

Here are possible celebrations:

- Work anniversary
- Employee's birthday
- A goal that has been reached if there was no set reward.

Awards for achievements and for relationship building:

- Labor percentage achieved
- Great review on social media

Jim and I also show appreciation by rewarding the whole crew. Sometimes it's a store party in the summer at a lake with a picnic and jet skis! In winter, it might be a Christmas party with games, great food, and fun gifts.

However, don't wait for the holidays. Especially when work has required some long hours, we reward everyone on the team with things like:

- Root beer floats or other fun foods.
- Breakfast casserole and homemade muffins.
- Gift certificates for coffees, movie passes, bowling gift cards.
- Uplifting notes on the Point of Sale System.
- Encouraging words on the employee-area board.
- Sprucing up an outside area where breaks are taken.
- Sometimes cold hard cash!

This kind of work culture retains great First Customer employees. Most of our managers are raised up from within this environment. We observed their buy-in and watched them developing leadership skills, which naturally led to them becoming managers. It has been much easier than hiring from outside the organization. A 30-minute interview cannot fully divulge what a person's work ethic and leadership skills will be. It is always a greater risk to hire outside. You have no way of knowing if that person will fit in with your culture and existing employees. Far better to promote those you have personally trained and promoted from within.

In several cases over the years, Jim and I were able to sell the business to a manager. I love when both parties win! Keep in mind that not all employees have management potential. Good worker does not always equal a good manager. Only elevate those who inspire people around them to be and do better.

So how did Jim and I find these incredible people? Great question. It's one we get asked all the time! Here's our top-secret strategy in a nutshell:

Whenever we have a current employee who is precisely what we want, we ask them if they have any friends that would fit our company. It's really that simple. First of all, birds of a feather flock together. A high-caliber person is likely to be surrounded by other high-caliber people. Second, we've found that most people really enjoy working with their friends. I can say that, after 38 years in business, the only time this doesn't work is if the employees are not emotionally healthy people. If they are sound in their judgment and have integrity, it is a terrific way to get employees.

So I guess our top-secret strategy isn't secret anymore. Feel free to implement it in your own business the next time you need to hire someone.

Don't Overlook Young People as Your First Customer

We've had great success by finding quality young people and training them, from day one, in our relationship-centered approach to business. In fact, it has been part of our mission for 25 years to be the first-choice job trainer for young people. Where do we find the cream of the crop? Through building relationships throughout our community.

We proactively connect with:

- Teachers, coaches, and other school employees.

- Moms who can recommend their former babysitters who are now ready for a job with a regular paycheck.

- The Chamber of Commerce will put the word out in monthly newsletters that you are looking for employees.

- Local Community Colleges. You can post on their websites and community boards.

- Youth pastors.

- Families whose older children have already proven to have a great work ethic.

- Customers! When they see the great work environment, they will want their kids to work for you!

The Interview System

Once you have quality candidates, you need to screen them to see if they are a good fit for your specific business and your available position. Find an interview system that fits the needs of your business. You can develop your own. But here are some essential elements:

1. Write down the questions before the interview.

2. Ask the exact same questions to each applicant.

3. Do not lead with your question. You want to discover who the candidate is, not talk about who you are or what you hope they are.

4. Consider not responding to their answers until the questions have all been asked.

5. For clarification to their answers, respond with: Tell me more, explain, give an example.

6. Use a scoring system. It is hard to remember all that you heard during the interview. Keep it simple like 1-4. 1 being a weak response and 4 a strong positive response.

7. Listen for words that describe traits you are looking for, such as responsible, hard-working, excellence.

8. Ask if they have any questions for you.

Scoring the answers given and looking for specific indicators that reveal their innate strengths also exposes areas that will be challenging for them. It has given us the ability to hire exactly who we need to fill staff openings.

The interview exposes how they will perform the tasks the job requires. As long as I rely on the interview, I acquire employees who enjoy the job and stay with the company for an above-average length of time.

Our industry calculated that the cost of a new minimum wage employee is $2500.00. It's worth hiring well. The opposite is also true. It can be very costly to have unhappy customers because of poor service. Not to mention the time and energy spent training someone to do a job that isn't a good fit for them.

How to Hire Well

Here are some helpful tips on how to hire well:

- Define the attributes of the position you are hiring for. Write out the perfect fit, detail-by-detail, for that position.

- Ask questions that would reveal those attributes without asking directly. For instance, if the job requires physical endurance and speed, asking what kind of hobbies the prospective employee engages in can reveal whether or not that person has high energy.

- If you are hiring for a position that involves lots of customer service, notice if the interviewee smiles and makes eye contact. You can seldom train a smile. You have to hire someone who is already smiling.

- Asking what the person plans on doing in the next two years may give you an idea if they will be around for that long.

- Ask the question, "If you could be anything you want, what three things would you really like to be and why?" You are looking for someone who desires to serve people in some capacity.

Orientation: Get Everyone on the Same Page

Once hired, the orientation sets the stage for what they can expect from you and what you expect from them. Information should be clearly stated in written form and given verbally to allow for

- Treat the new employee as a member of the work-family.

- Introduce them to the other First Customers and the regular customers.

- Show them around their new work environment.

- Assign a trainer to them (be sure to mention something they have in common as they begin their relationship).

- Using eye contact and a confident tone, assure them that you believe hiring them was a great decision.

Training Your First Customers

Positive traits like service, respect, fun, inclusivity, and appreciation are caught. When caught, they are repeated.

You should be training all employees every day, rotating the subject matter. Not only are there new employees who need to learn, but all of us need reminders and affirmations. Don't forget to talk about what people are doing *well* to encourage them.

The Company Handbook

The Company handbook is your training manual; it's also your how-to and your go-to book!

The handbook should include:

- State and Federal protections for the employee, which can be found on those websites.
- Safety regulations including all necessary work certificates necessary
- Scheduling, Dress code, Sick calls, paychecks, etc.
- Guiding Values Principles and Mission Statement.
- History of the business.
- Cultural language and communication within the organization.
- Any perks that come with the job, such as employee discounts.

- Job descriptions are clearly written for each position they are required to perform.

- A clear word picture of the steps to excellent customer service.

- How you want them to respond to customer complaints.

- Non-profits supported by the business

When A First Customer Doesn't Work Out

Not every hire will work out. If you are clear with your expectations and feedback, there are never any surprises. Spell out exactly what the process looks like for an underperforming employee. That way, when someone is let go, clear steps have been laid out, and they've been told exactly what steps are needed to improve performance.

Letting go of an employee is never easy and, in today's culture of entitlement and social media mobs, it can be fraught with problems. Fortunately, unpleasant terminations *can be a rare occurrence* if you keep the lines of communication open.

How do you do that? Simple: just ask another question!

The beauty of asking another question in conversations with your First Customer is to build the relationship. By showing sincere interest, you gain your employees' trust, and they come to respect your knowledge and wisdom. They may even see you as a mentor— in business and in life. And that's a beautiful foundation for the kind of long-term relationships that can help any business thrive.

Now Grow It

- Plan some rewards & celebrations
- Make a list of people and places who might be able to connect you to potential employees
- Nail down your interviewing system
- If you don't have one already, begin compiling a company handbook
- Develop a clear strategy for terminating employees who are not a good fit

CHAPTER 4:
Relationship Culture of Safe Space Communication

> *Do not let any unwholesome talk come out of your mouths, but only what is helpful for building others up according to their needs, that it may benefit those who listen.*
> *- Ephesians 4:29*

To build a healthy relationship with our First Customer, we need to create a work environment that is a safe space to work in. Yes, physical safety is important and necessary. So is the way communication is spoken and written.

Healthy Relationships Thrive in Safe Spaces

I had the privilege of working with a business consultant ten years ago. We set aside an entire week for our leadership team to work with him.

I thought he would inspect the stores, look at the Profit and Loss sheets. All he did was train on the subject of clear communication. It was all about safe space, clearly written job descriptions, and handbooks. We were amazed at the positive impact this one change has made in our business.

We knew if we wanted to create a "safe space" culture in the workplace, a great place to begin was in our own home. Jim and I started being more intentional about honoring one another. It was worth the effort and discipline. Romans 12:9-12 sums it up nicely: *"Love must be sincere... cling to what is good. Be devoted to one another in love. Honor one another above yourselves."*

Safe Space Communication

Following are eight powerful communication guidelines to ensure a safe environment characterized by respect and personal growth.

1. Facts-only when communicating.

   Non-debatable information that I/we can see hear, touch, experience. Avoiding "meaning-making," which is making a judgment concerning someone else that the facts may or may not point to.

2. My truth from my experience.

   There is no such thing as common sense. Be aware, when communicating information, that people come from different life experiences. Choose words appropriately. Common sense is only common if all parties come from similar experiences.

3. Intention/Impact

   There is often a difference between what you **intended** to do or communicate...and what was **actually** communicated or received. Intention is only effective when the desired impact has been made. When someone's body language tells you that you are not clearly understood, you can begin the conversion again. Take a different approach. Once again, asking questions will often clarify whether or not you've made the desired impact.

4. Introvert/Extravert

   Be aware of differences in how people process information or stress. Respectfully give time and space for a person to communicate. Do not dominate the conversation and do not keep your important, constructive perspective to yourself. Just because you think it doesn't mean you should say it.

5. Remember 7-45-48

Research indicates three distinct avenues of communication: 7% of what is communicated through words, 45% is communicated through body language, and 48% is communicated through tone. All three play an important role and should be used appropriately. If you say the right thing in the wrong tone, you have said the wrong thing.

6. Elephant in the Room

The "Elephant in the Room" is an unspoken concern that everyone knows exists. Communicate concerns respectfully, at an appropriate time, and don't keep them inside. By naming the Elephant, its power and size diminish, opening the door to clear communication.

7. Confidentiality

Create an environment where gossip is detested and not tolerated. Speak to the person involved. No one else.

8. "I" Statements

I take personal responsibility, and I do not blame. I speak for myself based on my data.

These eight clear communication skills create environments and cultures of respect and honor. Whether it is a spouse you work with, businesses you exchange services with, or First Customer employees. If you prioritize clear communication, you can spend your energy building your business instead of putting out "fires" or handling complaints.

Far too often, I'm guilty of making assumptions about why someone is behaving in a certain way. Then I find myself doubting the relationship. Asking one or two simple, kindly-directed questions can clear the doubt and bring movement toward each other.

Ask the question that moves the relationship toward each other.

This is building a business by building relationships.

Now Grow It

- Choose one person at home and one at work to implement one of these skills within a week.

- Continue working through the list.

- Find one other person who is willing to put these communication skills into practice. You both will be encouraged, and you will deepen the understanding of each skill. Talk about your progress at least once a week.

CHAPTER 5:
Relationship Culture of Learning Names

> *"Sometimes you wanna go where everybody knows your name."*
> *- Cheers theme song*

If you watched the famous sitcom Cheers, you surely remember how everyone who walked in the door was greeted by the entire bar calling out their name. That is exactly the culture we try to create in our businesses. That's because it is the best feeling in the world to *belong* and to be wanted.

Building a business by building relationships begins with learning someone's name. Remembering names takes effort, but the effort reaps great rewards. And for those who wisely have their eyes on the bottom line, it also builds sales. This is the Golden Goose of business.

We have contests to see who can learn the most names of our regular customers. We make it a game featuring rewards and prizes. Money talks! Find out something the First Customer wants. Set a goal for them to achieve.

Almost every business has a group of "regulars." In the case of our restaurants, a regular is a customer who comes in every week. Sometimes three times a week. They are now friends, not just customers. And friends market your business for you. They tell people, "Hey, I'm friends with the owner!" They celebrate birthdays with you. They bring in their friends or relatives when they visit (to impress them with what an *insider* they are!)

It is like multiplying your customer base times their influence.

How to Win Friends and Influence People

If you haven't read it yet, be sure to read Dale Carnegie's classic book, *How to Win Friends and Influence People*. If you've read it before, read it again. It's that important!

The stories will capture your attention. Here is what Carnegie says about the best way to get started in building relationships with people. It has been used in some of the largest and longest-lasting companies for decades. This is how you and your First Customer will achieve this.

Six Ways to Make People Like You

1. Become genuinely interested in other people.
2. Smile.
3. Remember that a person's name is, to that person, the sweetest and most important sound in any language.
4. Be a good listener.
5. Talk in terms of the other person's interest.
6. Make the other person feel important and do it sincerely.

I have a very personal story of a moment in my life as a 12-year old that shaped my future. I didn't realize its importance or significance until many years later. It literally set the course for what became my greatest strength.

I went to a party of girls from my Sunday School class. I was still very new in town as I had just moved from another state, away from all my family and friends. I came home in tears because no one had spoken to me the entire time. They stood in groups, not including me.

Instead of going to the teacher and complaining, my mother said to me, *"Remember how you feel at this moment. If it is in your ability when you see someone who looks like they are feeling alone and isolated just like you do now, reach out to them by making eye contact, smiling, and introducing yourself."*

I literally walked through the halls of junior high, high school, and everywhere I went making eye contact, smiling, and saying Hi! It made me popular and noticed when I was just wanting someone to feel *seen*…and not feel the pain or fear of missing out.

After reading *How to Win Friends and Influence People*, I began to work at learning people's names since it is a powerful way to form an instant connection.

I really noticed how well learning names built relationships when I was a grocery checker. My lines would be the longest because people wanted to be helped by someone who remembered their name.

Have you ever noticed how quick people are to say they can't remember names? They have just told their brain, *"Don't even try!"*

If you don't think it is important to remember people's names, think about a time when you met someone, then saw them again later. But they didn't recognize you. How did you feel?

If it's really true that a person's name is the most wonderful thing anyone can hear, why would we deny them the pleasure? Have you ever remembered someone's name, and his face lit up as he said, "You remembered!" The look on the other person's face tells you how much it means.

You could change your sales in a week if you and your First Customer began remembering the names of your second customers.

People think that the way to build sales is by finding new customers. New customers are great. But an even better way to build sales is by getting your regular customers to come back more often. And one key to making that happen is making sure *your business* is the place where everybody knows their name.

How to Remember Names

If you want to succeed, help people feel like they belong! Start by remembering names. Here's how:

- When you meet someone, and they tell you their name, repeat it back to them. It's not awkward when they know you are serious about remembering it. Sometimes I have them spell it if I am struggling to say it correctly. I will use it as I'm talking to them when it's appropriate. I repeat it again as I say goodbye.

- When you get to a place where you can write it down, you should also include something about them to connect to their name. You can use the Notes feature on your phone to store names and details about people you meet.

- Try to remember to repeat the person's name later that same day as you reflect on how pleasant the conversation was.

- Look for that person in the setting where you first met, so you can connect again.

You can do this! It is beautiful to connect with people. We are made to bring joy and life to one another. This one habit of learning names could change the course of your business.

More Practical Tips

Here are just a few more ideas:

- Before you go to a meeting or gathering, determine your plan of action to learn names and build relationships.

- Whenever you're in a new group setting, start talking to someone as soon as you enter the room. Don't let the awkwardness build in silence. That's not to say you have to be talking every moment, but it can set people at ease.

- Make eye contact with a smile on your face and say, *"Hi, I'm _____. Pleasure to meet you!"* Then make a statement about the subject that has brought together the meeting.

- Determine some subjects of interest you could turn into conversation. Make a list on your phone.

Give it a try this week. Promise yourself to look for someone to approach and begin a conversation as soon as you walk in the room. It's good for business, good for your brain, and good for your well-being. It will also build confidence in you. People like to be around confident people.

This is absolutely foundational for building a business by building relationships: learn people's names!

The tagline for our restaurant is *"Where Neighbors Become Friends."*

I'm reminded of a quote written in the journal of a 16-year old daughter of a friend—the young girl had passed away from leukemia. Afterward, her family found her philosophy of friendship scribbled on a page:

> *"I went out to find friends and struggled to find them. I went out to be a friend, and I found hundreds."*

This is another sowing and reaping principle that is true of all relationships. So often, we want what we are not willing to give. If we begin to sow kindness, generosity, and hospitality, we will also reap it. Galatians 6:7-9 states it plainly, *"Whatever a man sows, that will he also reap."*

What are you sowing in your relationships? With your First Customers? Second Customers? Community?

Now Grow It

- Determine to build a new relationship.
- Highlight someone at the next meeting you attend.
- With a smile and eye contact, introduce yourself and start a conversation.
- Practice your best listening skills as they talk.
- Greet them consistently using their name when you see them again. If you've forgotten their name, just say, "I really want to learn your name. Could you help me by repeating it again?" How could we not feel important with that said?

CHAPTER 6:
Relationship with Community

What good is it, my brothers, if someone says he has faith but does not have works? Can that faith save him? If a brother or sister is poorly clothed and lacking in daily food, and one of you says to them, "Go in peace, be warmed and filled," without giving them the things needed for the body, what good is that? So also faith by itself, if it does not have works, is dead.
- James 2:14-16

Which would you rather have? 1,000 customers or 200 regular customers?

I'll pick the 200 regular customers. I can have a relationship with the 200.

The number one need of businesses is building repeat customers because 80% of your business comes from 20% of regular customers. Why do you think that is? Because people like to go where they are recognized and greeted with a smile. That makes them feel valued.

Which customers do you spend the majority of your time and resources on? Fishing for new customers or taking care of the ones you already have?

In a brick-and-mortar business, the customers are people in the community where you live. Where you shop and get your car washed. Where your children go to school. Where you go to church. Where you play together in hobbies or days off.

The people you do life with every day are potential customers!

You don't have to market your business to them. Just be genuinely interested in other people. Remember: People do business with people they like, know and trust! That's exactly what a relationship is all about!

Even though I'm now writing about *our* business experience, for many years, it seemed like *my husband's* business. That's the way I saw it. I didn't feel like I could play an important role in it. I know that there are other married couples like us, where it took a while to get buy-in from the spouse who isn't as involved in the day-to-day aspects of the business. That was me for the first 16 years.

You know what got me involved?

There was a significant downturn in the economy. It was October of 1997. Business was flat. Two major businesses on the same street as ours both closed: one next door and one across the street. These businesses provided large foot traffic to our business. We experienced a 30% decrease in sales as a direct result of their closing.

Jim and I got scared!

We put our dream home on the market *(just in case)*. We prayed and asked God for direction. The next day, I was at a business that I had never been to before, and I happened to meet the owner. She and I got to talking, and she invited me to a meeting of other business owners through an organization called LeTip. It was very similar to the Chamber of Commerce, except that there was only one business of a kind in each business category. There were 98 businesses that all exchanged goods and services with each other. It was all based on relationships—with businesses in the same community supporting each other.

Becoming a member of LeTip helped sales slowly increase as all these new friends became new customers.

What an answer to prayer! At the same time, we woke up to the reality that it was up to us to be proactive about marketing the businesses in the neighborhoods and towns of each of the stores. We had to admit that we had become tired and bored, and it was showing in our work.

Spending time with other businesspeople got me energized. And I finally realized that my penchant for building relationships could make a significant difference in our business.

I learned so much from the members. My fellow LeTip members taught me:

- How to approach people to make a sale.
- How to make business fun, not always serious.
- The value of a relationship in doing business with someone you see every week.
- The power of referrals.
- The benefits of getting honest feedback from business-minded people who have your best interests at heart.

Even now, 20 years later, I go to a doctor I met at LeTip. Same with my hairdresser. Do you know how much money she has earned just from me over 20 years? I don't want Jim to figure that one out. Those 98 members of LeTip were all potential marketers for my business, and I did the same for them. Everyone wins through strategic partnerships and word-of-mouth marketing.

By building relationships with all of these business owners, I created a steady stream of *repeat customers* for our business. And not just any customers! These are customers who pro-actively send more customers our way. Of course, we do all we can to turn those customers into repeat customers, too.

The moral of the story? Our business not only survived the market downturn, it thrived. And I never again viewed our business as *"my husband's thing."* Yes, he still does what he does best, but now I see the value of doing what I do best. We're better together.

Is it possible that someone in your business already has a knack for relationship building? Now is the time to send them out into the community to pro-actively put that skill to work.

Community Involvement

Decades ago, we were inspired by the story of a business that experienced explosive growth through community involvement. They constantly came up with fun ideas, from hosting extravagant floats in their local parade to hosting fundraisers for local sports teams. Earlier in the chapter, I admitted that we had become tired and bored with our business. Well, not anymore! We latched onto this idea, and it revolutionized everything. Suddenly, business wasn't all tedious labor; instead, it became energizing and exciting.

Marketing through community involvement is still one of our top strategies. Community is our number one value in the business, and we make it our goal to be a light in the community. It also yields a lot of "fruit" and spreads your name around town.

Work doesn't have to be drudgery. It can be fun again and engaging. Even though I was the one most involved in community activities, my husband and managers are fully supportive. Opportunities will present themselves when you determine to be a positive influence in your community. For example, several years ago, one of our employees was in a serious bonfire accident. She and another woman were burned over half of their bodies. Our manager asked if we could have a fundraiser. Jim and I decided to give every cent from a whole day towards this. People in town heard about it and told us we would be swamped. Former employees offered to work for free that day to help. School employees offered to work. A woman from the local paper found musicians to play all day long next to the business, creating an atmosphere where the community could gather with the families of those injured. I will never forget that day.

The fundraiser to help these community members would never have become the success it did without all the relationships we built over time. Past employees from many years prior. School lunch ladies who were customers of the business cut vegetables and made pizza dough. Local churches where employees attended announced the fundraiser at their services. Businesses, such as the local newspaper, offered support by putting out ads about the fundraiser free of charge.

When planning, don't be afraid to just ask the question, "Where can I help?" You don't know until you ask. It takes someone to get the ball rolling, and that someone could be YOU! Your business can make an impact on your community just as we did in ours.

Now Grow It

- Join your local Chamber of Commerce. If it does not have a strong membership, find a service club (*such as Rotary, Lions Club, etc.)* with a healthy membership.

- Choose a service club in your community (such as those listed above) and attend regularly. Make sure you are meeting a new person each week.

- When you are with business members in your community, be sure you ask questions! Keep the questions relevant. Think of questions that require more than a one-word answer.

- Remember to take note of names and exchange business cards.

- Track your current number of customers and watch them grow as you begin building relationships.

Enjoy making some new friends in your community!

CHAPTER 7:
Relationship with Professionals & Purveyors

> *"Commit to the Lord whatever you do, and he will establish your plans."*
> *- Proverbs 16:3*

Building a business takes several teams of people, including a team of professionals.

Too often, business owners don't gather the needed support team until they have a significant problem. A support team is there to prevent the problem. Your professional team may include:

- Attorney: Contracts, wills, litigation, employee practices.
- Accountant: corporate structure and tax issues.
- Insurance agent: business and liability coverage.
- Advertising agencies
- Fire Marshal
- Health Inspectors
- Commercial real estate agent

Jim and I made this mistake. We had no idea what we were getting ourselves into when buying our first business. In the beginning, sales were great, and there was more money than we had ever seen before. Neither of us understood cash flow or taxes. At the end of the year, we were informed of a large tax bill including unpaid obligations to social security on behalf of our employees. This was serious!

Our ignorance caused unneeded stress. We learned the hard way that a business budget is just like a personal budget. If you spend everything you make each month, you'll be in trouble when an unexpected expense comes. And there are always unexpected expenses. We hadn't considered that unexpected business expenses are usually much larger than anything we'd encountered in our personal lives.

In our first business, some of the money was spent on inspirational wall decor for our office and professional sporting event tickets, to name a few things. These purchases weren't illegitimate business expenses. We took staff to sporting events – and we talked about business on the way there and coming back. It was all part of building relationships to build our business.

The issue was the timing in making those purchases. While we were busy inspiring our employees, we hadn't fulfilled our basic tax obligations. Worst of all, we didn't have a substantial emergency fund in the bank.

When we got the news about how much we owed, we were tempted to panic. Our first accountant had simply *assumed* we knew all about our tax liability, and we didn't know what we didn't know, so we didn't ask the right questions. In the end, the accountant helped us create a plan to pay off the large sum of taxes owed in an acceptable time for the IRS.

Even though it was a colossal mistake of grave importance, we continued a business relationship with that accountant for several more years. Then he made another significant mistake. That's when we hired another accountant, who had been recommended by some business associates. He helped us find a bookkeeper who has been with us ever since. We've had that same accounting firm and bookkeeper for more than 20 years. Sometimes it takes several relationships before you find the one that is a good fit for both parties.

Back to the story where these professional relationships of necessity began.

If we had invested the money upfront, hiring the right accountant and a good attorney, we would have saved a lot of money and hassle in the long run. We would have set up the correct type of corporate structure, and it would have been set up with a clear understanding of how taxes were taken correctly out and distributed. We also would have been spared the fear and overwhelming doubts about our ability to achieve our goals in business.

Fortunately for us, we were able to weather that storm relationally and financially. Many businesses do not. One reason might be because they can't find the help they need to lead them out of their situation. Another reason might be that the stress is more than they can emotionally handle.

The relationship with these professionals is very personal. Make sure you get trusted recommendations from those who have successful businesses. Interview potential professional team members just like you would potential employees. If you don't connect with them, move on to another one. Make sure it's someone you feel can be trusted implicitly. If you're going to work closely with them and they're going to know your business inside and out, you should enjoy and appreciate their time and feedback.

It's also important to vet your relationships with your core professional team through the lens of integrity. There are laws, and then there are ethics. They don't always line up. Just because something is LEGAL, doesn't necessarily mean it is ETHICAL.

Jim asked our attorney, Joel Pearsall, at the beginning of our business, *"That is the law, but is it ethical?"* He was taken aback by Jim's sense of ethics. Joel had never been asked that question before. I think it came from Jim reading the Book of Proverbs many times. It teaches that the fear of God *(respect of His laws)* is the beginning of wisdom. The relationship between Jim and Joel went to a deep level of mutual respect and admiration. He left his law practice to become the president of Northwest Nazarene University. But beforehand, he made a professional recommendation and left us in good hands with our current attorney.

Hiring the right professionals is a vital part of wise business stewardship. Good stewardship is rewarded by God. The Bible says, *"From everyone who has been given much, much will be demanded; and from the one who has been entrusted with much, much more will be asked"* (Luke 12:48b). Jim has taken this seriously during nearly 40 years in business and in our 45 years of marriage, as well.

All these professionals on your team will deal with important aspects of your business. God's favor on your life and business can make a big difference in a critical moment. That favor comes from recognizing and abiding by the governmental laws of the land and spiritual laws.

Each of the professionals can be wise counsel for your business. For instance, accountants tell you where you have been. They can help you with records that are important for the IRS. But using *only* past information is like driving while looking in the rear-view mirror. It is dangerous and costly to make decisions looking backward. You also need to ask them for forward-thinking cash flow statements to project income, profit, and expenses. Most accountants won't do this if you don't ask. So as always: just ask another question!

Building Relationships with Professionals

Here are some tips on how to build a relationship with your professional team, so they can help you build your business and protect it:

- Be friendly and likable.
- Communicate promptly, not at the last minute.
- Speak to them with appreciation for their help.
- Write down your questions in advance, so their time is not wasted.
- Avoid peak business seasons if possible.
- Be honest and don't hide information out of fear or embarrassment.
- Be kind during inspections.
- Ask about them and things important to them.

Your Team of Purveyors

A purveyor is a person who sells or deals in particular goods: vendors, suppliers, retailers, etc. These are the people and businesses that provide you with everything you need to stay in business. We've been talking about having customers, but in this case, you are the customer!

If you're like most people, you only communicate with purveyors when you have a problem with them or their service. You and I depend on their goods and services but rarely compliment them for on-time deliveries or the myriad things they do, often on a daily basis, to keep our doors open for business. They are people, too, and respond favorably to respectful relationships. So don't be like most people; instead, be the one customer who makes their day by treating your purveyors like valued business partners.

Building great relationships with your purveyors can save time, money, and peace of mind — allowing you to focus on building your business.

One of the big issues with purveyors is getting credits for missing or damaged products. I'm sure you are very quick to mention it when that happens. But what about those rare instances when the purveyor accidentally gives you *more* than you paid for? Are you as quick to mention that? If you communicate with them when they give you something they *didn't charge you for*, they will likely trust you when you ask for a credit.

Employees watch this kind of interaction, noticing fair and just practices in your business dealing.

Shouldn't our employees notice that we operate with integrity toward everyone?

So how can you and I build pro-actively build relationships with purveyors?

- When short on cash, make them the first person you pay, not the last. Business screeches to a halt without them.
- Be consistently honest about their deliveries.
- Be loyal to them. If you're going to shop around, tell them.
- Market for them to other businesses. Help them grow.
- Communicate appreciation.
- Ask them a question about their family or hobbies.

Building a business by building relationships also means being the kind of customer who's a pleasure to work with. Jesus said it best when He gave us The Golden Rule, *"So in everything, do to others what you would have them do to you"* (Matthew 7:12).

Now Grow It

- Set an appointment with one of your professional teams this week.
- Email or call a sales representative sharing your appreciation for them.
- Compliment your delivery driver for what they do well.

CHAPTER 8:
Relationship with God

> *"Then Jesus came to them and said, 'All authority in heaven and on earth has been given to Me."*
> *- Matthew 28:18*

> *"I have given you authority."*
> *- Luke 10:19,20*

I have been in relationship with God through trusting Jesus Christ as my Savior and Lord since I was 13 years old. I knew of God. I remember seeing the "life-size" picture of Jesus the Good Shepherd, with the little children gathered around him, on my mom's preschool Sunday School classroom wall. My Grannie, who spoke tenderly and lovingly about God, had two pictures of Jesus in her home. One was of his face, and one was Jesus knocking on a door. As a family, we prayed before meals and when we were afraid. My parents always began their prayer with, *Father, thank you for this privilege of prayer.* These family members, Sunday School teachers, and youth pastors showed me who Jesus is.

When I was at church camp, I heard a pastor share James 2:19, *"You believe that there is one God. Good! Even the demons believe that–and shudder."* I knew at that moment that I had not trusted and exchanged my life for His indwelling presence in me.

Believing means to trust in His death on the cross for my sins (as well as the sins of everyone for all time) in exchange for His life in me through the power of the Holy Spirit. Believing is trusting in what He did and receiving it as mine. His righteousness for my sin. That is one business exchange outweighing anything ever sold:

> *"For it is by grace you have been saved, through faith-and this is not from yourselves, it is the gift of God-not by works, so that no one can boast."*
> *- Ephesians 2:8,9*

> *"For God so loved the world that whoever believes on Him should not perish but have everlasting life."*
> *- John 3:16*

As a Christian businessperson in the marketplace, I do well to operate in the Spirit of Christ, who is all truth, wisdom, and love. According to 2 Peter 1:3, God gives me all I need for life and godliness: *"His divine power has given us everything we need for a godly life through our knowledge of him who called us by his own glory and goodness."*

This relationship with God through Christ and His Word is priceless. His Word is my personal handbook for all I do. When my relationship with God is unhindered, He can then shine through me in my relationships with others.

The Priority of God's Word

Most of the time, when I have my quiet time, I have music playing as I read the Bible and pray. I have grown to love just listening to music as I am quiet. If I'm rushing through a morning, I might skip Bible reading. I love to study, but if I'm not careful, it can slip for a while. I recently came across this thought, and it has really captured my attention:

"Worship brings feelings, but without the Word to ground those feelings, we will not have the commitment or strength to hold out for victory when the storms shake our foundations."

Life can knock you down! Business can be like a boxing ring at times. You and I need the power of the written Word of God to release its wisdom, might, and strength in us with revelation of its meaning.

The Bible is meat to the soul. Our worship, then, is the offering for what was received. Here's how Psalm 19:7-11 puts it:

"The law of the Lord is perfect, refreshing the soul. The statutes of the Lord are trustworthy, making wise the simple. The precepts of the Lord are right, giving joy to the heart... in keeping them there is great reward."

There is so much in the Bible concerning how to live in a way that is full of wisdom, knowledge, and loving relationships – especially in Paul's letters to the churches. Praying, reading and meditating, then journaling about it, are how a relationship with God is built.

During my freshman year, the president of our college would speak once a week during chapel. Almost every single week, he used Psalm 1 as his text:

> *"Blessed is the man who does not walk in the counsel of the wicked... his delight is in the law of the Lord...He is like a tree planted by streams of water, which yields its fruit in season...Whatever he does prospers."*

We all love the promise, *"Whatever he does prospers."* But take a moment to notice that there is a prerequisite for that promise. God has a part, but we have a part, too. Our part is walking in God's counsel and delighting in God's law as we meditate on it. Jim and I have memorized this Psalm, and we keep it at the forefront of our hearts and minds. Still today, we pray and seek God's wisdom whenever we make decisions that affect our business and those connected to it.

The Importance of Tithing

If you want to transform your life and business. If you want to see God's favor surrounding you like a shield. If you want to prosper and enjoy financial blessing, here's the best business advice you'll ever receive: tithe.

God's promise concerning the tithe is stated plainly in Malachi 3:10:

> *"Bring the whole tithe into the storehouse, that there may be food in my house. Test me in this," says the LORD Almighty, "and see if I will not throw open the floodgates of heaven and pour out so much blessing that there will not be room enough to store it."*

I know, I know. Most business books are all about getting. But as Christians, we understand the power of giving. Not just giving to our customers, employees, and community. But giving our first and best to God. We've already established that giving him the first moments of our day is the surest way to make wise decisions and enjoy a prosperous life. But the Bible makes it abundantly clear that how we handle money reveals more about the condition of our heart than almost any other thing we do. Jesus talked more about money than any other topic. More than heaven, more than healing, even more than love.

Money matters. In fact, the one area where God says, "Put me to the test," is in the area of our finances.

Write this in a prominent place until it is written on your heart:

Not everything you earn belongs to you.

The first 10% of everything you earn belongs to God. Period. End of discussion.

Everything you are, everything you have — including your business — it's all a gift from God. It belongs to Him. He's just lending it to you for a season. Eternal rewards are beyond the scope of this book, so let's just talk about ROI. And let's give ourselves a simple mathematical reality check. Which of the following do you think will yield a better return?

100% minus God
Or
90% multiplied by God

You don't have to be a math whiz to solve that particular equation. If you want God at the center of your business, pay him what he is owed: 10%. If I had a business partner with unlimited power and influence who promised to work with me every day for the rest of my life, and all he wanted was a 10% stake, I would take that deal any day of the week (and twice on Sundays).

We are absolutely amazed at the level of favor and blessing we have seen in our personal lives and in all of our businesses. And we are entirely convinced that tithing is a big reason why God has poured out his favor on us. It will be the same for you and your business. God will bless your finances when you tithe to Him through your local church.

There is so much wisdom in Scripture to learn and apply to business. Another favorite verse on wisdom is, *"If any man lacks wisdom let him ask of God who gives to all men liberally without finding fault"* (James 1:5). God never tires of us asking Him for wisdom in any and all situations. Ask often! Keep a dialogue going with Him all day. Once again, remember our maxim: just ask another question. It applies to your relationship with God, too.

Seeking God's Guidance

Imagine having the smartest person in the world as your personal business advisor? How valuable would that be? Imagine if that advisor was on retainer, on-call 24/7/365. How often would you ask for their input? My guess is: constantly!

Mary Geegh was a single missionary in India during the early 1900s, when there weren't nearly as many resources or channels of communication as we enjoy today. Her needs often had to be met by God in supernatural ways. She wrote the following prayer, and it has been a great prayer for us many times. Don't miss the last sentence.

God Guides By Mary Geegh

Father, I come to you in the name of Jesus Christ, Your Son, and according to James 1:5, I am seeking wisdom for _____.

In the name of Jesus, according to Matthew 28:18 and Luke 10:19&20, I take authority over Satan and his fallen angels and command that they be rendered deaf, dumb, and blind to my prayers and removed from my presence.

I place my own voice under subjection to the shed blood of Jesus and command that my own thoughts be taken captive to the obedience of Christ, according to 2 Corinthians 10:5.

I ask Father that only Your Holy Spirit will speak to me as I wait on you for wisdom, insight, and direction for _____. [Whatever] You show me and direct me to do, I will quickly obey. Amen.

I really want to encourage you as a Christian businessperson to live a life set apart to God for his service. Bring Him into your business. Seeking His wisdom and direction will bring so much peace and joy to doing business. He knows all things present and things to come.

This relationship affects all other relationships; none is more important.

Now Grow It

- Set aside time daily to pray, read the bible, meditate, and journal.
- Read Psalm 1 every day for a month.
- Consider committing the entire passage to memory. It's well worth the effort.
- Tithe to your local church.

CHAPTER 9:
Relationship with Self

> *"I praise you, for I am fearfully and wonderfully made. Wonderful are your works; my soul knows it very well."*
> *- Psalm 139:14*

Building healthy relationships starts with yourself. You must like yourself in order for someone to like you. Remember, people do business with people they know, like, and trust. Our relationship with ourselves is highly complex, and we'll break up this chapter into different sections to reflect that complexity. We need to discuss self-talk and personal discipline.

Self-Talk

I think most of us, until trained differently, have more negative than positive conversations with ourselves. These conversations have a lot to do with words that have been spoken to you by teachers, coaches, pastors, siblings, parents, and grandparents. These conversations shape your emotions, thoughts, beliefs, and actions.

Joyce Meyer sums it up nicely in her book, *Power Thoughts: 12 Strategies to Win the Battle of the Mind*:

> *Whatever you hold in your mind will tend to occur in your life. If you continue to believe as you have always believed, you will continue to act as you have always acted. If you continue to act as you have always acted, you will continue to get what you have always gotten. If you want different results in your life or your work, all you have to do is change your mind.*

Here's an exercise that's sure to be enlightening. For one week, make notes about your internal dialogue. Write down what you say to yourself. Now imagine if the person you care about most spoke those words aloud to you. How would it make you feel? Better or worse? Empowered or defeated? The words on that page might solve more than one mystery about your life!

Maybe it's time to start thinking about what you're thinking about.

For a year, it was my goal to take every thought captive. I knew perfection was impossible in this task, but I was determined to become intentional and conscious of what I was thinking. I knew it would make a difference in my relationship with myself and with those around me.

I had no idea how much I was getting in the way of my business success – or the way my relationships were being negatively affected. Then one day, my daughter kindly said, *"Mom, you are your own worst enemy."*

I am my own worst enemy, and you are your own worst enemy. And that's how it will stay until we make a conscious decision to think and believe differently. Your mindset determines the path you are on. Your failure to master your mindset affects you, your family, your employees, and your community. Likewise, your success benefits you, your family, your employees, your business, and your community.

Change your mind, change your life. Start by noticing what goes through your mind. Then do whatever it takes to think differently about yourself and your life.

Personal Discipline

"All discipline is not pleasant yet painful. But for those who would be trained by it will yield peaceful fruits of righteousness."
- Hebrews 10:25

For your business to succeed, you need to be able to count on...you. You need to be reliable. And that requires personal discipline.

Of course, you require the best from your employees and other business professionals, but your business will never be all it can be unless and until you require the absolute best from the person in the mirror. Your first step is recognizing what's not working and why then putting in the hard work of discipline to make the necessary changes.

I love how Craig Groeschel puts it: *"Discipline is choosing what you want most over what you want now."* Couldn't have said it any better!

I came to a point in my life where I was absolutely determined to pursue what I wanted most, even when it meant letting go of what I wanted at the moment. I chose to address areas in my life that needed intentional changing. As a result of those efforts, I eventually became a healthier, more balanced person who could better serve my relationships.

Here are my **Top 5 Tips To Improve Your Relationship with You**:

1. Create Routines

It takes discipline to stick to a morning and evening routine. With all the responsibilities of owning a business, routines can give consistency and rhythm to your weekly schedule.

Physicians who work with Olympic athletes have found that sleeping between 10pm and 6am produces the deepest rest. Take note of that, night owls! Studies have also found that turning off blue light *(such as computers, TVs, and cellphones)* helps sleep come easier and more quickly.

Sample Morning Routine

5:00	Hot water with lemon
	Quiet time: read, pray, meditate
6:00	Exercise while listening to goals and affirmations recorded my phone.
6:30	Shower and dress
7:00	Breakfast

Evening Routine Sample

7:00	Stop eating for the day
9:00	Turn off all electronics
	Prepare clothes and bags for the next morning
	Write 3 things you accomplished today in your journal Brush, floss, read
10:00	Turn out the light

You may already be doing some of this. But if you've never established a solid routine, this can be life-altering. Sleep is when our bodies refuel, so we are ready for the next day. I am my best and most productive self when I follow these routines, especially when I regularly write down three things I accomplished that day. It is motivating for me and encourages me to complete something that has been weighing on my mind.

2. Choose Your Focus

At the beginning of each year, I prepare with a 21-Day Focus. You can do this any time of the year!

At the beginning of the 21-Day Focus, I write a list of 100 things I want to be, do and have. Then I turn it into a personal mission statement and make a vision board reflecting those goals and priorities. I always do this with a group of friends online, so we can hold me accountable. We check in every day during those 21 days. Accountability is key. The women in my group are an answer to prayer; they are my iron sharpening iron relationships.

No matter what else I'm focusing on, I always keep the morning and evening routines front and center. That's because I've learned that, without those routines, I'm unlikely to accomplish my other projects.

Here's how to do the 21-Day Focus:

- Start either an evening or morning routine for three weeks. If you are highly motivated, do the steps below as well.

- Write a list of 100 things you want to be, do, and have in your life and business.
- Create a Vision Board with the top 5 things for your business this year.
- Write a business mission statement.
- Live this out with an accountability group of like-minded business people.

3. Learn to Rest

Every part of our being needs regular times of rest. I define rest as *ceasing from work to allow refueling*. Our souls need solace. Rest doesn't mean sleep. You might find more rest for your soul by taking a hike along a creek. Or a bike ride to a park. Go to a place outside your regular routine. Take in beauty as though it was created just for you to enjoy.

An excellent way to rest is to play. Any hobby that brings satisfaction relieves stress. Having something you enjoy *outside your business* will fuel you to work more productively when you are at work.

Johnson O'Connor Research Laboratories in Seattle, Washington, found that if people regularly participated in a hobby they really enjoyed, they could more easily endure a job that was not their first choice.

My daughter went through three days of testing to see which careers – and what kind of college – was a good fit for her personality. The test suggested she should incorporate a hobby that included small motor skills. As a result, she made jewelry. It was very satisfying for her as she used creativity in color and design to creating something beautiful with her hands.

Why not find a hobby that interests you and do it for a few hours each week?

4. Walk in Humility

Walking in humility takes discipline because it requires us to remember who God is and who we are. That doesn't come naturally to any of us. We like to play God – telling ourselves that we are in control, we are judge and jury of the universe, and we can figure everything out if we think about a problem long enough.

But humility means maintaining a teachable spirit no matter who you are with in conversation. It means learning from others and not assuming your way is the only way or even the best way.

I have had people drive a considerable number of miles for business advice...then not listen to a word I say. I politely listen to their ideas, plans, and vision, patiently waiting for the moment when they are ready to listen. Instead, many times the person is too busy trying to convince me of why they are right. They want to list all the reasons why they are sure their ways are better. At the end of the consultation, it's obvious that they haven't even considered the information and experience I have to offer.

So why drive all that way...just to hear themselves talk?

It has been painful to watch people lose thousands of dollars *(and sometimes their entire life savings)* because they didn't really want advice. They wanted confirmation that they were right, and they weren't willing to consider another perspective.

How much better off these people would have been if they had simply chosen to walk in humility, acknowledging that no one person has the inside track on everything. That's why we need each other; and why we need God. The Bible warns us that "Pride goes before destruction, a haughty spirit before a fall" (Proverbs 16:18).

So unless you want to fall – *and maybe even see your business fail* – keep pride in check with humility. Discipline your ears to hear and your heart to yield. Be willing to learn something from everyone you meet. A great way to do that is to talk less and listen more.

One thing that has helped me is constantly reminding myself that God is God and I am not! He is perfect and worthy of my worship. So I choose to spend less time thinking about myself and my circumstances, and more time thinking about Him and how far above my circumstances He is.

Worship is one of those activities that requires humility. Remember the quote I shared earlier:

> *"Worship brings feelings, but without the Word to ground those feelings, we will not have the commitment or strength to hold out for victory when the storms shake our foundations."*

Being honest with our fears requires a place of humility as well. It shows that I don't have it all together or the strength in times of weakness.

There was a time in our business when Jim was feeling overwhelmed and defeated. He asked me, *"Will you love me and want to be with me if I lose everything?"* My answer came from deep within me, *"You didn't have any of this when I married you."* He needed to know that it was him I was committed to and not the wealth that he produced. Jim got back to work!

Say every morning after you brush your teeth, "You are God and I am not! Today I will learn from you and from everyone around me."

5. Work Hard...But Not Too Hard

There is no way of getting around it; business requires hard work, especially anytime you start something new. Whether it's a new business or a new initiative within an existing business. You don't know what you don't know. (There's that humility thing again!)

Even with great preparation, there can be variables you never even considered. I remember years ago, on a very stressful day, reassuring myself that the doors would shut for the night and quiet would come. So I could figure out what had to be done the next day to not repeat the horrors we had just endured.

A disciplined pursuit of personal development has a wonderful effect on all the relationships in our lives. There is a reward for good, hard work. There are also negative consequences if we take it too far and become workaholics. The key is balance. That's what the first four tips in this list are designed to help you maintain.

When I can present my healthiest self in spirit, soul, and body, I am free to focus on the people around me. When my relationship with myself is healthy, I have the energy to build my business by building relationships. Freedom is a beautiful thing. Freedom to be me gives me the freedom to love you for who you are.

Now Grow It

- Which of these areas of self-care will you begin to implement?
- Write a plan of action to begin the change.
- Set the date to begin.
- Measure and track progress.

CHAPTER 10:
Relationship with Spouse and Family

> *"How good and pleasant it is when God's people live together in unity!"*
> *- Psalm 133*

I doubt if anyone would argue that spouses and family are the most important relationships of our lives. I also know that they can be the ones who often are neglected when I am stressed in my business.

There is hope!

This is how Jim and I included our children and worked through our relationship challenges. The children grew up with business being a part of their lives. They helped to do all kinds of things at the stores at really young ages. They got to be with employees and us. They folded boxes, wiped tables, swept the floor, and kept our employees company. Holidays were hectic, and they worked right alongside us.

Making it fun!

If you're including your children in your business, find ways to make it fun for them to get involved. For our kids, washing dishes wasn't so bad when there was loose change in the sink for them to find when they got to the bottom. Here are other ideas to get your family involved in the business:

- Reward quickly when children are young.
- Verbally affirm how much help they are, especially when speaking to others about them.

- Have special toys that stay at the business, so they look forward to them.

- Have treats on the way home after work. It can be time at a park or an edible treat.

- Support their endeavors, whether it's a school project, sports, or practicing a new skill.

- Kids make great marketers in t-shirts with business logos (think about their little league sports teams wearing them).

- Include them in company parties and let them invite a friend or cousin to be their guest.

- Include them when you give gifts to the employees.

- Take the family along to conventions instead of leaving them at home. Take a babysitter if needed. Make sure to have some family time while at the convention.

These are just some of the things we did with our kids, but don't be afraid to get creative! There are so many fun things you can do to include your children in your business. Our Christmas parties were a blast with games and extravagant food. The gift exchange was entertaining because we conducted it like an auction. The employees *(and our kids)* traded and schemed to get the one they really wanted, and we bought gifts with people in mind knowing that's what would happen. The kids helped decorate the house, wrap gifts, and prepare the food. They greeted guests and took coats at the door.

The summer parties we have are at lakes, with jet skis and boat rides. Everyone brings their famous summer salads, and we make sure there are plenty of food and drink choices. Our kids helped us host these gatherings, making sure everyone got turns on the jet skis and boats. They also helped entertain the children who came with their parents.

Our kids enjoyed being a part of any gathering with our employees because they knew them as an important part of their lives. They got teased like any older sibling would do with a little brother or sister.

All three of our kids became employees of our business when they turned 16. Two of them got counseling notices (i.e., reprimands) from their bosses. The managers clearly understood that the owners' kids did not have any special privileges; they were treated like every other employee. The managers also knew it was their store to run and manage as they saw fit. The manager did not have to put up with any nonsense from the owner's kids. The two that got counseling notices were sometimes "testing" their manager or us, their parents.

Our kids knew and understood that while at times it was all-consuming for mom and dad, the business provided a lifestyle that was something they were proud of. We had a huge buy-in from them because they understood, from an early age, that the business made fun things possible.

When Family Members Work Together

Here are some tips to keep in mind when family members work in the business:

- Children must respect those in authority in the workplace.

- Support the manager and supervisors, making it clear that they have the right to lead family members.

- Encourage open and honest dialogue about their behavior.

- Use data, not judgment, when discussing disagreements.

- Be slow to speak and quick to listen to all parties.

- If you get positive feedback about a family member, communicate that, too!

- Use discernment to help build positive relationships between family members and their managers; look for ways to build bridges.

- Teach your child to work hard and lead those working with them so that they are a genuine asset to their managers.

- Hold family members to the *same* standards everyone else is held to. Be careful about being too harsh or making excuses for them. This will build trust with the whole team.

As entrepreneurs, Jim and I talked about business a lot around the kids. The subject came up at the dinner table, on road trips, and when we were with other families that were themselves self-employed. All three of our adult children have been sharing with us their memories of the 400-mile road trip we used to take to their grandparents' house. I would often read to Jim from business books on these trips. Or we would listen to business audios the entire way. The kids listened to all this business language and wisdom. They absorbed much more than what we realized.

I never thought twice about them being business partners with us. Jim had hoped that might happen because he saw excellent customer service skills in all of them. However, it's not something we pushed for or even talked about. Neither Jim nor I followed in the career paths of our parents, so we never assumed our kids would want to be in the same occupation that we were in.

Our oldest son, towards the end of his senior year in college, was getting engaged. He had been studying Business Economics and getting restless about what his future might be. One day during a conversation with Jim, Zech, our son, asked if there might be an opportunity in our business. We told him a business like ours, over two hours away, was for sale. We went to look at it. What we saw was a lot of untapped potential. Untapped potential is like throwing a ball across a room in front of a dog. Jim being the dog.

Jim asked Zech if he wanted to take his fiancé and look at the community and opportunity and consider whether they were interested in partnering in it. Our daughter-in-law, Rachel, agreed to make the drive and contemplate what life there would be like. She was graduating in education and would be able to find a teaching job almost anywhere. They decided to make a life together two and a half hours away from both sets of parents and make it independently. After their third year in business, they were named Business Owners of the Year.

Child number three, Reuben, had made his way in the construction world and had become a foreman. He was thriving in what he was doing. At that same time, Jim and I decided to build a larger business than we had previously done. We thought it would be the pinnacle of our years in business. We discussed decisions we were making concerning the business with all three kids because we all liked to dream and plan. Sometimes dreams and plans take a while for us to grow into them. What ended up happening was all three kids saw that we were in over our heads – and in trouble – at the soft opening. The only marketing we had done was to start a Facebook page.

At the grand opening, we had 1700 friends. The two boys worked the weekends to give us a hand. They then called their sister and told her how overwhelmed Jim and I was. She was a customer service expert with a successful serving career in Southern California. She had been drafted to be the head server at a restaurant listed in *Wine and Restaurant* magazine; the restaurant had also won Zagat's award for *Restaurant of the Year* in Los Angeles. Six months pregnant, leaving a toddler behind across the country, we flew her in to help as well.

Reuben came to us just two weeks into the business and said he had two dreams on consecutive nights about Jim and me. He concluded, *"I think I'm supposed to be working with you in this business."* We asked if he had talked it over with his wife. He said yes, and she, too, believed he was supposed to work with us. That was six years ago. Reuben is a terrific General Manager and part-owner in this business as he brings a skill set we did not have. We couldn't have done it without him and the other two kids *(all in their 30's)* who came to our rescue in time of need.

The relationships Jim and I have with our children were always interwoven with our faith in God and the vision we shared for our family life together. Everyone understood that our business supported our dreams and created our livelihood.

We knew children were a gift given by God. We knew we were responsible for raising them to love and honor God and His ways and model good stewardship of all we owned. Relationships with them were built as we shared our hobbies and helped them discover their strengths. We loved them unconditionally, and we were vulnerable and honest about our weaknesses.

Our parenting was usually filled with lots of teaching. Both Jim and I taught and led Bible Studies. We both have degrees in Bible, so it was natural to share our knowledge. The teen and early adulthood years had some tough challenges relationally with all three of them. Most were caused by underlying issues that went unhealed and unresolved. Sometimes, those issues led to rebellious actions. Jim and I prayed for them to get caught if they had destructive behavior going on. And they did.

Sometimes Jim and I had great grace and calm in the moment, and sometimes we did not. By God's grace, we kept pursuing the relationship, and over time, grace won! Family Counseling helped. Jim and I took a class based on *Parents in Pain* by John White. Another tremendously helpful book was the book, *Families Where Grace is in Place* by Jeff VanVonderen.

I believe that God designed healing to take place in relationships. Shame wants us to run away from each other. Grace says *I need God's mercy too*. Those traumatic experiences were healed through counseling and lots of dialogue, tears, and forgiveness. They also drew us closer and deeper in our relationship with each other. Learning to deal openly with our personal relationship issues has made it that much easier to confront business issues. We still have moments when emotions run hot, but we seem to get through them quicker than we used to.

Phrases to Improve Family Communication

A few phrases that have helped us work through business issues that can trigger strong emotions are:

- "The story I am telling myself is…"
- "I need you to be my dad right now."

- "Mom, minimize the task right now." *(I can sometimes overwhelm my partners.)*
- "We will talk about this later; let's get through this issue right now."
- "Give me some time to think about it."
- "Who owns the problem?"
- "What's the question?"
- "Stick with the data!"
- "Time to check our priorities in regards to _____ and come to a consensus."
- "Let's celebrate and mark this win."

Obviously, it takes a lot of honest communication to include your family in your business. It takes authenticity that can be brutally painful. But the end result can be deep endearment when the relationship takes priority over the business, as it should. We recognize that not everyone wants to include family members in their business. For our family, however, it's been a tremendous blessing.

Making Marriage Work When You Work Together

I shared in Chapter One how helpful it was to learn about our contrasting personalities. While we deeply loved each other, our differences were vast. We had gone through premarital counseling, which helped. Who can teach it all? There is so much to learn about marriage. For the two of us, we could sweep most disagreements "under the rug" with our busyness. We read books and tried to apply what we learned.

Nevertheless, the year of our 21st anniversary was one of the most stressful:

- All three kids were teenagers, and none were thriving.
- My mom passed away suddenly.
- The economy was in trouble.
- The same business that was once booming was suddenly floundering.
- We put our dream home on the market to sell.

Jim heard a relationship counselor on the radio who had just written a book, *How Can We Light a Fire When the Kids Are Driving Us Crazy?* The author, Ellen Kreidman, also had a companion audio teaching series, which we ordered immediately. The help was super-practical. I don't think there had been anything written at that point by Christian authors who talked about the communication struggles between husband and wife on such a practical level.

As a result of the teaching, Jim became intentional in his words, patient and attentive to my needs. He responded calmly to my fiery frustrations. I could no longer fight with him because he wasn't fighting back. It was an answer to prayer. Our marriage was healing, slowly but surely.

I learned that men feel the need to fix the issues that the wife talks about. I'm a verbal processor, so I was unintentionally overwhelming him with issues to fix. And he was already overwhelmed with work and family issues. But I also felt overwhelmed by his attempts to *fix me* when all I really wanted was to feel *heard*.

Ellen suggested that when a spouse needs to process something, let the other person know that you're not asking them to fix anything. You just need them to be a sounding board. I would see Jim's posture relax in the chair and, even though I was sharing problems, he was able to remain at ease, rather than springing into fix-it mode.

This teaching was gold!

She also suggested a standing weekly date with a pre-scheduled babysitter. That was huge. We even had a favorite restaurant we always went to, so we didn't have to stress about deciding where to go.

The other thing that kept a connection between Jim and me was something pretty special. Before I let you in on our secret, would you like to know some other marital tips that helped us?

Top 4 Marriage Tips

Realize that you see situations differently. Just like there are two sides to a penny, each person has their point of view. Neither is right or wrong. Embrace the differences. Learn your spouse's method of processing or decision-making so you can be patient and appreciative. I love the scenario told of the couple who wanted to go to the top of the Empire State Building. One wanted to run the stairs, the other wanted to take the elevator. The solution? They celebrated the view together at the top instead of trying to get there the same way.

1. When you make a decision, and it turns out to be the wrong one, just make another one. Decision-making can be a lot of pressure. This is true in business as well as in a marriage. Communicate and agree on a new plan.

2. Always speak respectfully of your spouse's gender. Have you been in a conversation with other people when someone refers to the opposite gender with disdain? It has been a socially acceptable form of teasing for too long, ignoring the damage it can subtly instill in an insecure person. God created man and a woman in His image and said it was very good.

3. Here is the tip I was holding out on you. I even shared it with a group of married missionaries in Africa who found it helpful in their relationship. What if you could make a connection with your spouse that would enable both of you to let go of the rush of the day and briefly center in on just each other? Well, there is a way. It's the 7-second kiss! Not two seconds. That just says, ok, you're home now go do such and such. No, it's got to be seven seconds. That's because seven seconds is just enough time to make a genuine connection and to surrender your attention solely to each other.

4. We had a house for nine years with a large enough pantry with a door that we would just go in there. It was wonderful because we reassure each other that we thought of them during the day and were glad to be together again.

Whether you work with your spouse or your kids, or both, nurturing strong relationships with your family members is at the very heart of building your business.

Employees Have Families, Too

Most of our employees have spouses and families as well. You will rarely have an employee who doesn't have someone they go home to when they get off work. You should care about those family relationships, too

Among the most important of those relationships is the spouse of your key employees. For example, if the spouse is hounding your manager to get home while you are pressuring him to stay a little later, you put that employee in an impossible position. Either way, they end up feeling like they've let someone down. You can help by setting clear expectations during the hiring process and by having clear job descriptions. Those job descriptions need to include the manager's responsibility when the unexpected happens.

Some managers recognize that they can alleviate being home later than expected by training other people to be in charge when they are not there. Our best managers worked themselves out of a job, developing their crew to work and take care of customers even when the manager isn't there. Employees who are proud to work in your business want to do their part. They want the business to be successful because that makes them feel important.

They should also know how and when they will be rewarded if profits increase. Do you want someone whose eye is on the clock? Or do you want someone who will help build your business and participate in the profit and growth? The solution is simple: make sure everyone is invested in the overall success of your business. When you share the rewards, people are more willing to share in the required sacrifices.

Building a Relationship with Your Employee's Spouse

Whenever possible, build your business by building relationships with the spouses of key team members. Here are some practical tips that have helped us:

- Take them out to dinner together.
- Invite them to company parties.
- Remember their birthday with a gift.
- Send Christmas cards to them.
- Write letters of appreciation.

One of the smartest things you can do is make expectations clear during the interviewing process. Some businesses even include spouses in the last part of the interview when hiring.

We have had managers in the past who did not have buy-in from their spouses. They seldom worked out long-term. Part of the problem was that the requirements and opportunities of the job were never shared with the spouse. That's why getting to know them, either during the hiring process or soon after that, can benefit everyone.

Now Grow It

- Which ideas can you implement if you still have children at home?

- Any strategies to apply with family members who work in your business?

- Make a list of ideas you want to try in your relationship with your spouse.

- Don't forget about that 7-second kiss!

- Write a letter of appreciation to spouses of key employees.

Conclusion

Building a business by building relationships adds great value to all people involved. Whether it's within the four walls of the business or outside, building connections drive businesses that grow and are sustainable. All people benefit as collaborative relationships expand reach and impact.

Here's a recap of some of the key points we've shared:

- Relationships with people are the key to building your business!

- Know yourself and make it a high priority to get to know the people around you.

- Respect each personality type as you navigate business relationships.

- Spend as much energy on your First Customer (employees) as you do on paying customers.

- Continually sharpen your safe space and clear communication skills.

- Learn people's names. Make it a game and become great at it!

- We are all placed in communities with a purpose to accomplish. Support the community by sowing seeds of generosity.

- Tell your customers regularly how much you appreciate their business.

- Assemble your professional support team today. Assess who you are missing and seek out referrals from business people you respect.

- Show appreciation to your purveyors. Watch the excellent service they will give to you in return.

- Meet with God every day. He is waiting for you. Take good care of yourself because you are His reflection.

- Remind your family that your relationship with them is the most important relationship you have.

Building a business by building relationships is a rock-solid strategy for creating a prosperous, sustainable business. It gives purpose to the calling of being a business owner. Whether you own a business now or are thinking about it for the future, I hope you found valuable help and lots of hope on these pages. I pray blessings over each one reading this book.

In Him,

Paula Newman

Pay It Forward

As a business owner, I'm a firm believer in the power of paying it forward. If this book has opened your heart and mind or given you fresh encouragement in your business, please take a moment to help the next business owner who needs this information.

You can do that just by sharing a brief testimony of how this book helped you and/or how you can envision applying these principles to help build your business by building relationships.

Just visit: Review.JimandPaula.biz

On behalf of the businesses that will prosper based on your recommendation, thank you!

Special Thanks from Paula

To my teacher, business partner, and husband of 45 years. Thank you for leading me by example on how to gently guide people who choose to work with us in our businesses. Your "Jimisms" will long ring in their hearts and minds, as they do mine. You have the broadest shoulders of any man I know. I am blessed you chose me!

So thankful for the next generation who will stand on my shoulders and keep building businesses. Daniela, Zech, and Reuben, I have the highest respect for who you are as business leaders. You have grown beyond your dad and me. Keep the next generation interested in business as a God-given calling. To our future leaders, wherever God should lead, Zoe, Luke, Hope, Lincoln, Selah, Abigail, and all to come along, I will forever be your cheerleader!

To my Bible Study group, *The Devoted Doves*, your prayers and commitment to Jim and me as we sought to follow God's leading in our 60's has given us the encouragement to keep dreaming with God. Love you each one.

To Donna Partow, Tamera Aragon, and the RLC gals, your support and accountability to get God's

Message to the world have been a dream come true. The internet was useful in some pretty wonderful relationships with you all. I look forward to more exciting journeys together.

My Chamber of Commerce family, thank you for the relationships and memories. Your devotion to helping businesses has certainly helped me.

About Jim & Paula Newman

Jim and Paula Newman have been in business for almost 40 years. Having met in Bible College, they assumed they would go into full-time ministry. But when they purchased a brick-and-mortar business, they instantly discovered their true calling as relationship-centered business leaders.

Their love for people is most frequently expressed through local community involvement. But they've also taken short-term mission trips to Africa and Israel and have helped open businesses in the United Arab Emirates.

The Newmans have three married children and six grandchildren. They live in the Pacific Northwest, where they enjoy hiking, biking, kayaking, hunting, and fishing.

Made in the USA
Monee, IL
09 June 2023